SPANISH FOR BEGINNERS

Angela Wilkes
Illustrated by John Shackell

Designed by Roger Priddy
Edited by Nicole Irving
Language Consultant: Manuela Gomez

CONTENTS

2 About this book
4 Saying "Hello"
6 What is your name?
8 Naming things
10 Where do you come from?
12 More about you
14 Your family
16 Your home
18 Looking for things
20 What do you like?
22 Table talk
24 Your hobbies

26 Telling the time
28 Arranging things
30 Asking where places are
32 Finding your way around
34 Going shopping
36 Shopping and going to a café
38 The months and seasons
40 Colours and numbers
41 Pronunciation guide
42 Grammar
44 Answers to puzzles
46 Glossary

About this book

Going abroad is much more fun if you can speak a little of the language. This book shows you that learning another language is a lot easier than you might think. It teaches you the Spanish you will find useful in everyday situations.

You can find out how to . . .

talk about yourself,

and your home,

count and tell the time,

say what you like,

find your way around

and ask for what you want in shops.

How you learn

Picture strips like this show you what to say in each situation. Read the speech bubbles and see how much you can understand by yourself, then look up any words you do not know. Words and phrases are repeated again and again, to help you remember them.

The book starts with really easy things to say and gets more difficult towards the end.

New words

All the new words you come across are listed on each double page, so you can look them up as you go along. If you forget any words you can look them up in the glossary on pages 46-48. *If you see an asterisk by a word, it means that there is a note about it at the bottom of the page.

Grammar

Boxes like this around words show where new grammar is explained. You will find Spanish easier if you learn some of its grammar, or rules, but don't worry if you don't understand it all straightaway. You can look up any of the grammar used in the book on pages 42-43.

Internet links*

At the top of each double page you will find descriptions of useful websites for learning Spanish. For links to these sites, go to **www.usborne-quicklinks.com** and enter the keywords **spanish for beginners**.

Puzzles

Throughout this book there are puzzles and quizzes to solve (see answers on pages 44-45). You can also find picture puzzles to print out on the Usborne Quicklinks Website at **www.usborne-quicklinks.com**

Practising your Spanish

Write all the new words you learn in a notebook and try to learn a few every day. Keep going over them and you will soon remember them.

Ask a friend to keep testing you on your Spanish. Even better, ask someone to learn Spanish with you so that you can practise on each other.

Quiero...

Try to get to Spain for your holidays, and speak as much Spanish as you can. Don't be afraid of making mistakes. No one will mind.

* For more information on using the Internet, see inside the front cover.

Saying "Hello and Goodbye"

The first thing you should know how to say in Spanish is "Hello". There are different greetings for different times of day. Here you can find out what to say when.

In Spain it is polite to add **señor**, **señora** or **señorita** when you greet people you don't know. You say **señor** to men, **señora** to women and **señorita** to girls.

Saying "Hello"

This is how to say "Hello" to your friends.

This is more polite and means "Have a good day".

This is how you say "Good evening" to someone.

Saying "Goodbye"

Adiós means "Goodbye".

These are different ways of saying "See you again".

Saying "Goodnight"

You say "Buenas noches" in the evening and at bedtime.

Hola, Marisa, ¿cómo estás?

Muy bien, gracias.

Hasta la vista, Pedro.

Hasta pronto.

How are you?

Hola, ¿cómo estás?

This is how to greet someone and ask how they are.

Hola, ¿cómo estás?

Muy bien, gracias.

This person is saying that she is fine, thank you . . .

Buenos días, ¿cómo estás?

¡No muy bien!

. . . but this one is saying things aren't too good.

¿Cómo estás?

This list shows you the different ways of saying how you are, from very well to terrible. What do you think each of the people here would say if you asked them how they were?

muy bien	very well
bien	well
bastante bien	quite well
no muy bien	not very well
muy mal	terrible

5

What is your name?

Here you can find out how to ask someone their name and tell them yours, and how to introduce your friends. Read the picture strip and see how much you can understand. Then try doing the puzzles on the page opposite.

New words

yo	I
tú	you
él	he
ella	she
ellos	they (male)
ellas	they (female)
¿cómo te llamas?	what are you called?
¿cómo se llama él/ella?	what is he /she called?
¿cómo se llaman ellos/ellas?	what are they called?
yo me llamo	I am called
él se llama	he is called
ella se llama	she is called
ellos/ellas se llaman	they are called
¿quién es?	who is that?
es	that is
mi amigo	my friend (male)
mi amiga	my friend (female)
¿y tú?	and you?
sí	yes
no	no

Ellos and ellas

There are two words for "they" in Spanish: **ellos** and **ellas**. When you are talking about boys or men, you say **ellos** and when you are talking about girls or women, you say **ellas**.

If you are talking about boys and girls or men and women together, you say **ellos**.

Buenos días, ¿cómo te llamas?

Mario, ¿y tú?

Yo me llamo Alicia.

Introducing friends

Es mi amigo. Se llama Pedro.

¿Quién es?

Es mi amiga. Se llama María.

¿Cómo se llaman?

Se llaman Pablo y Juan.

What are they called?
Can you answer these questions in Spanish?

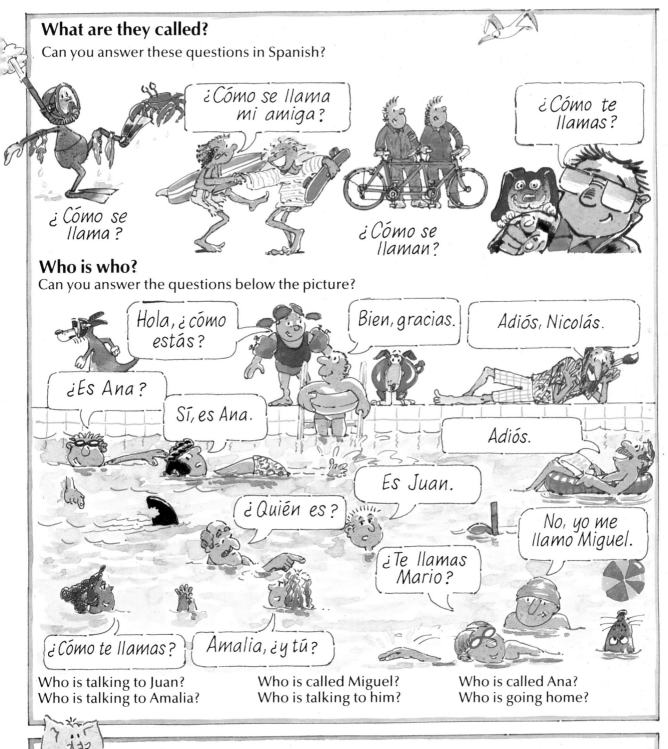

Who is who?
Can you answer the questions below the picture?

Who is talking to Juan?   Who is called Miguel?   Who is called Ana?
Who is talking to Amalia?   Who is talking to him?   Who is going home?

Can you remember?

How would you ask someone their name?
How would you tell them your name?

You have a friend called Amalia. How would you introduce her to someone?
How would you tell someone your friend is called Daniel?

Finding out what things are called

Everything on this picture has its name on it. See if you can learn the names for everything, then try the memory test at the bottom of the opposite page. You can find out what **el** and **la** mean at the bottom of the page.

la chimenea

el tejado

el Sol

el pájaro

¡Buenos días!

el nido

el árbol

la ventana

la flor

la casa

Esta es mi casa.

la puerta

el garaje

la verja

el gato

el perro

el coche

El and la words*

All Spanish nouns are either masculine or feminine. The word you use for "the" shows what gender the noun is. The word for "the" is **el** before masculine (m) nouns and **la** before feminine (f) ones. It is best to learn which word to use with each noun. "A" or "an" is **un** before **el** words and **una** before **la** words.

el Sol	sun	**el nido**	nest	**la ventana**	window
el árbol	tree	**el pájaro**	bird	**la puerta**	door
el tejado	roof	**el garaje**	garage	**la flor**	flower
el gato	cat	**el coche**	car	**la casa**	house
el perro	dog	**la chimenea**	chimney	**la verja**	fence

*The word for "the" is **el**, and not the same as the word for "he", **él**, which has a stress mark. You can read more about stress marks on page 41.

Asking what things are called

Don't worry if you don't know what something is called in Spanish. To find out what it is just ask someone **¿qué es esto?** Look at the list of useful phrases below, then read the picture strip to see how to use them.

¿qué es esto?	what is that?
es . . .	that is . . .
también	also
en español	in Spanish
en inglés	in English

Can you remember?

Cover up the opposite page and see if you can name all of these things in Spanish. Don't forget to say whether they are **el** or **la** words.

Where do you come from?

Here you can find out how to ask people where they come from. You can also find out how to ask if they speak Spanish.

New words

¿de dónde eres?	where do you come from?
soy de	I come from
¿dónde vives?	where do you live?
vivo en ...	I live in ...
¿hablas ..?	do you speak ..?
hablo ...	I speak ...
un poco	a little
español	Spanish
inglés	English
alemán	German
este/esta es	this is (m/f)
nosotros/as	we (m/f)
vosotros/as	you (plural, m/f)
ustedes	you (polite)

Countries

Alemania	Germany
Inglaterra	England
Francia	France
la India*	India
Escocia	Scotland
Austria	Austria
España	Spain
Hungría	Hungary

Where do you come from?

¿De dónde eres?

Soy de Inglaterra.

¿Dónde vives?

Vivo en Londres.

¿De dónde eres?

Soy de Alemania.

Mi amiga es de Francia. Vive en París.

Do you speak Spanish?

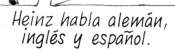

¿Hablas español?

Sí, un poco.

¿Hablas español, Lola?

Sí, hablo español y un poco de inglés.

Heinz habla alemán, inglés y español.

10   *The names of all these countries are feminine, but you normally only use la with India.

Who comes from where?

These are the contestants for an international dancing competition. They have come from all over the world. The compère does not speak any Spanish and does not understand where anyone comes from. Read about the contestants, then see if you can tell him what he wants to know. His questions are beneath the picture.

Angus viene de Escocia.

Estos son Marie y Pierre. Vienen de Francia.

Hari e Indira vienen de la India.

Yuri viene de Hungría. Vive en Budapest.

Franz viene de Austria.

Esta es Lolita. Viene de España.

Where do they all come from?

Where does Franz come from?
What are the Indian contestants called?
Is Lolita Italian or Spanish?

Is there a Scottish contestant?
Where do Marie and Pierre come from?
Who lives in Budapest? Where is Budapest?

Verbs (action words)	**singular**		**hablar**	to speak	**venir**	to come
Spanish verbs change according to who is doing the action. Verbs ending in **ar** follow the same pattern and have the same endings as **hablar**. You will have to learn **venir** by itself.*	I	yo	**hablo****	speak	**vengo**	come
	you	tú	**hablas**	speak	**vienes**	come
	you (pol)*	usted	**habla**	speak	**viene**	come
	he/she	él/ella	**habla**	speaks	**viene**	comes
	plural					
	we (m/f)	nosotros/as	**hablamos**	speak	**venimos**	come
	you (m/f)	vosotros/as	**habláis**	speak	**venís**	come
	you (pol)*	ustedes	**hablan**	speak	**vienen**	come
	they (m/f)	ellos/ellas	**hablan**	speak	**vienen**	come

 ## Can you remember?

How would you ask someone where they come from?

Can you say where you come from?
How do you say that you speak Spanish?
How would you ask someone if they can?

*You can find out more about verbs on page 43, and about polite (pol) forms on page 30.
Note that, in Spanish, you often don't need to say "I", "you", "she", etc. So, both **yo hablo and **hablo** mean "I speak".

More about you

Here you can find out how to count up to 20, say how old you are and say how many brothers and sisters you have.

To say how old you are in Spanish, you say how many years you have. So if you are ten, you say **Tengo diez años** (I have ten years).

New words

¿qué edad tienes?	how old are you?
Tengo cinco años	I am five years old
¿tienes...?	have you...?
tengo	I have
no tengo	I have no
el hermano	brother
la hermana	sister
casi	almost
ni	nor
pero	but

Plural words

Most Spanish nouns add an "s" in the plural (when you are talking about more than one person or thing), e.g. **hermano, hermanos.** Those nouns ending in a consonant add "es", e.g. **ciudad, ciudades.** In the plural, the word for "the" is **los** for **el** words and **las** for **la** words.

Numbers**

1	uno/una	11	once
2	dos	12	doce
3	tres	13	trece
4	cuatro	14	catorce
5	cinco	15	quince
6	seis	16	dieciséis
7	siete	17	diecisiete
8	ocho	18	dieciocho
9	nueve	19	diecinueve
10	diez	20	veinte

How old are you?

¿Qué edad tienes?

Tengo doce años, ¿y tú?

Yo tengo once años.

Have you any brothers and sisters?

¿Tienes hermanos?*

Sí, tengo un hermano y una hermana.

¿Qué edades tienen?

Mi hermano tiene diez años y mi hermana tiene nueve años.

Yo no tengo hermanos.

*When you ask someone **¿Tienes hermanos?** this means "Have you any brothers or sisters?"
**You will find a complete list of numbers on page 40.

Internet link For a link to a website where you can meet a Spanish family and improve your language skills with online activities, go to **www.usborne-quicklinks.com**

How old are they?

Read what these children are saying, then see if you can say how old they all are.

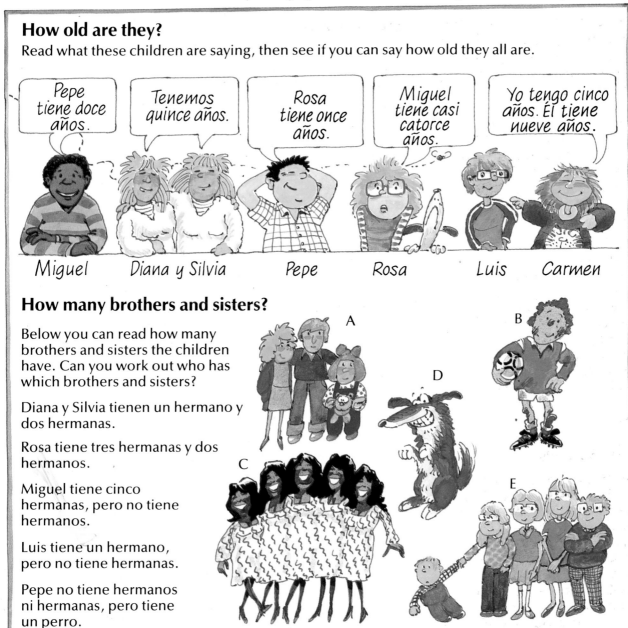

Pepe tiene doce años.

Tenemos quince años.

Rosa tiene once años.

Miguel tiene casi catorce años.

Yo tengo cinco años. Él tiene nueve años.

Miguel   Diana y Silvia   Pepe   Rosa   Luis   Carmen

How many brothers and sisters?

Below you can read how many brothers and sisters the children have. Can you work out who has which brothers and sisters?

Diana y Silvia tienen un hermano y dos hermanas.

Rosa tiene tres hermanas y dos hermanos.

Miguel tiene cinco hermanas, pero no tiene hermanos.

Luis tiene un hermano, pero no tiene hermanas.

Pepe no tiene hermanos ni hermanas, pero tiene un perro.

Useful verbs

tener	to have
yo tengo	I have
tú tienes	you have (singular)
usted tiene	you have (polite)
él/ella tiene	he/she/it has
nosotros/as tenemos	we have
vosotros/as tenéis	you have (plural)
ustedes tienen	you have (pl polite)
ellos/ellas tienen	they have (m/f)

ser*	to be
yo soy	I am
tú eres	you are (singular)
usted es	you are (polite)
él/ella es	he/she/it is
nosotros/as somos	we are
vosotros/as sois	you are (pl plural)
ustedes son	you are (polite)
ellos/ellas son	they are (m/f)

*Ser is used on the next page, so it may help you to learn it now.

Talking about your family

On these two pages you will learn lots of words which will help you to talk about your family. You will also find out how to say "my" and "your" and describe people.

Esta es mi familia.

mi perro

mi abuelo

mi padre

mi hermana

mi tío

mi gato

mi abuela

mi madre

mi hermano

mi tía

Who's who?

¿Es tu hermano?

Sí, es mi hermano.

Y ésta, ¿es tu hermana?

Sí, se llama Natalia.

¿Estos son tus padres?

¡No! Estos son mis abuelos.

New words

la familia	family	**la tía**	aunt	**delgado/a**	thin
el abuelo	grandfather	**los abuelos**	grandparents	**viejo/a**	old
la abuela	grandmother	**los padres**	parents	**joven**	young
el padre	father	**alto/a**	tall	**rubio/a**	blond
la madre	mother	**bajo/a**	short	**moreno/a**	dark-haired
el tío	uncle	**grueso/a**	fat	**cariñoso/a**	friendly

How to say "my" and "your"

The word you use for "my" or "your" depends on whether you are talking about a singular or plural word.

	my	your
singular words	**mi**	**tu**
plural words	**mis**	**tus**

14

Internet link For a link to a website where you can listen to a Spanish conversation about families and play some vocabulary games, go to **www.usborne-quicklinks.com**

Describing your family

Mi padre es alto y mi madre es baja.

Mi madre es alta y mi padre es bajo.

Mi tío es grueso y mi tía es delgada.

Mi abuelo es muy viejo. Yo soy joven.

Mi hermana es rubia. Mi hermano es moreno.

Mi perro es cariñoso.

Describing words

Most Spanish adjectives change their endings depending on whether they are describing an **el** or **la** word. They end in "**o**" in the masculine form, and this changes to "**a**" in the feminine form.*

Can you describe each of these people in Spanish, starting **Él es …** or **Ella es..**?

*In the word list on page 14, you can see adjectives in the masculine form, followed by the "a" for the feminine, e.g. **alto/a**. So the feminine is **alta**. You can find out more about adjectives on pages 42-43.

Your home

Here you can find out how to say what sort of home you live in and where it is. You can also learn what all the rooms are called.

New words

o/u*	or
la casa	house
el apartamento	small flat
el piso	large flat
el castillo	castle
en la ciudad	in the town
en el campo	in the country
a la orilla del mar	by the sea
papá	Dad
mamá	Mum
abuelito	Grandad
abuelita	Granny
el fantasma	ghost
¿dónde estás?	where are you?
el cuarto de baño	bathroom
el comedor	dining room
el dormitorio	bedroom
la sala de estar	living room
la cocina	kitchen
el vestíbulo	hall
arriba	upstairs

Where do you live?

¿Vives en una casa o en un apartamento?

Vivo en una casa.

Vivo en un piso.

Vivo en un castillo.

Town or country?

Vivo en la ciudad.

Vivo en el campo.

Vivo a la orilla del mar.

16   *You only use **u** before words beginning with "**o**" or "**ho**".

Where is everyone?

Papá comes home and wants to know where everyone is. Look at the pictures and see if you can tell him where everyone is, e.g. **La abuelita está en la sala de estar**. Then see if you can answer the questions below the little pictures.

Mamá   Papá   Abuelito

Abuelita   Pedro   Isabel

Simón   el fantasma

Yo estoy arriba.

Yo estoy en el dormitorio de Isabel.

Yo estoy en el cuarto de baño.

Yo estoy en la sala de estar.

Yo estoy en el dormitorio.

Yo estoy en la cocina.

¿Dónde estáis?

Yo estoy en el comedor.

¿Quién está en el comedor?
¿Quién está en la cocina?
¿Quién está en el cuarto de baño?
¿Quién está en el dormitorio?

¿Dónde está la abuelita?
¿Dónde está el fantasma?
¿Dónde está el perro?
¿Dónde está Pedro?
¿Dónde está papá? (Look at the word list)

Can you remember?

How do you ask someone where they live?
How do you ask whether they live in a house or a flat?

Can you remember how to say "in the country"?
Can you remember how to say "in the town"?

How would you tell someone you were upstairs?
How would you tell them you were in the kitchen?

Looking for things

Here you can find out how to ask someone what they are looking for and tell them where things are. You can also learn lots of words for things around the house.

New words

buscar	to look for
algo	something
hámster	hamster
encontrar	to find
lo	him/it
sobre	on
debajo de	under
detrás de	behind
delante de	in front of
entre	between
al lado de	next to
la alacena	cupboard
el armario	wardrobe
la butaca	armchair
la cortina	curtain
la planta	plant
el estante	shelf
la mesa	table
la alfombra	carpet
el sofá	sofa
la televisión	television
el teléfono	telephone
el jarrón	vase
¡aquí/allí está!	here/there it is!

¿Él or ella?

There is no special word for "it" in Spanish. You use **él** or **ella** ("he" or "she") depending on whether the word you are replacing is masculine or feminine. You use **él** to replace masculine words and **ella** to replace feminine ones.

¿Esto es para **el** hámster?
Sí, es para **él**.

¿Esto es para **la** tortuga?
Sí, es para **ella**.

The missing hamster

¿Buscas algo?

Busco mi hámster. ¡No lo encuentro!

No está sobre el armario.

No está debajo del sofá.

¿Está detrás de la cortina?

No.

¡Aquí está! ¡Entre las plantas!

In, on or under?

Try to learn these words by heart. **Al lado de** changes to **al lado del** when you put it before an **el** word, e.g. **al lado del sofá** (next to the sofa).

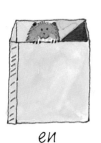

en *detrás de* *delante de* *al lado de* *debajo de* *sobre*

Where are they hiding?

Señor López's six pets are hiding somewhere in the room, but he cannot find them. Can you tell him where they are in Spanish, using the words above?

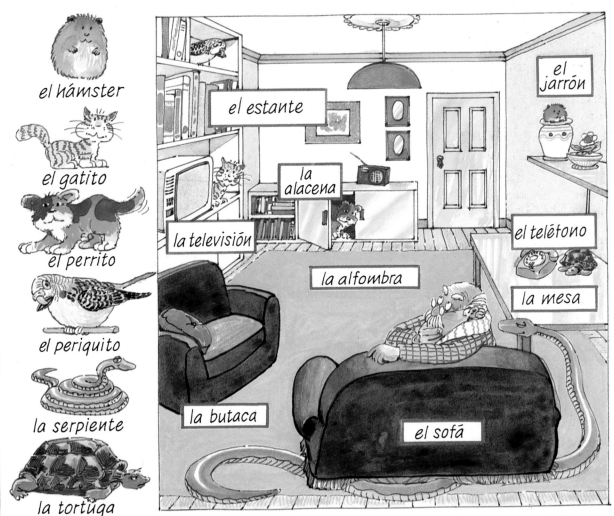

el hámster

el gatito

el perrito

el periquito

la serpiente

la tortuga

el jarrón

el estante

la alacena

la televisión

el teléfono

la alfombra

la mesa

la butaca

el sofá

19

What do you like eating?

Here you can find out how to say what you like and don't like.

New words

¿le/te gusta?*	do you like?
me gusta	I like
no me gusta**	I don't like
¿qué . . ?	what . . ?
me encanta	I love
en absoluto	not at all
entonces	then
mucho	very much
lo que más	the most
preferir	to prefer
sobre todo	best of all
la ensalada	salad
el pescado	fish
las patatas fritas	chips
el pastel	cake
la salchicha	sausage
el filete	steak
los espaguetis	spaghetti
comer	to eat
la pizza	pizza
la hamburguesa	hamburger
el arroz	rice
el pan	bread
el queso	cheese
yo también	me too

What do you like?

¿Le gusta la ensalada?

No, no me gusta la ensalada.

¿le gusta el pescado?

No, ¡No me gusta en absoluto!

¿Qué le gusta, entonces?

Me gustan las patatas fritas.

¡Y me encantan los pasteles!

What do you like best?

¿Qué le gusta más?

Me gustan mucho las salchichas.

. . .Pero prefiero el filete.

. . . Y me gustan sobre todo los espaguetis.

20

*Among friends, you ask "¿te gusta..?" but to be more polite, you would ask "¿le gusta..?"
**You can read more about negatives on pages 42-43.

What are they eating?

¿Qué comes?

Como una pizza.

Ella come patatas fritas.

Él come pan y queso.

Nosotros comemos hamburguesas.

Vosotros coméis arroz.

Ellos comen plátanos.

Who likes what?

Who likes cheese? Who doesn't like ham?
Who prefers grapes to bananas?

Can you say in Spanish which things you like and which you don't like?

A mí también, pero no me gusta el jamón.

Juan

Me gustan los plátanos.

Simón

Yo prefiero las uvas.

Me gusta el queso.

Jaime

Abuelito

Me gusta sobre todo la tarta de frutas.

Isabel

el jamón   la mantequilla   la tarta

el pan   la ensalada   los tomates   el queso

los plátanos   las uvas   una tarta de frutas   el zumo de naranja

---

Me gusta, me gustan*

Where in English we say "I like", the Spanish say "(it) pleases me": **me gusta**, or "(they) please me": **me gustan**.

me gusta/gustan	I like
te gusta/gustan	you like
nos gusta/gustan	we like

*In the same way, to say "I love/like a lot", you say **me encanta** followed by a singular word and **me encantan** followed by a plural.

21

Table talk

Here you can learn all sorts of useful things to say if you are having a meal with Spanish friends or eating out in Spain.

New words

a la mesa, por favor	come to the table, please
tengo hambre	I'm hungry
yo también	me too
sírvete	help yourself
servíos	help yourselves
buen provecho	enjoy your meal
¿me puedes pasar . . .	can you pass me . . .
el agua	water
el pan	bread
el vaso	glass
¿quiere usted* . . . ?	would you like . . . ?
más . . .	some more . . .
la carne	meat
sí, por favor	yes, please
no, gracias	no, thank you
he comido suficiente	I've had enough
¿está bueno?	is it good?
está delicioso	it's delicious

Dinner is ready

¡A la mesa, por favor!

Tengo hambre.

¡Yo también!

Sírvete, por favor.

Gracias.

¡Buen provecho!

¡Buen provecho!

Please will you pass me . . .

¿Me puedes pasar el agua, por favor?

¿Me puedes pasar el pan, por favor?

¿Me puedes pasar un vaso, por favor?

22   *Usted is a polite way of saying "you". You can find out more about it on page 30.

Would you like some more?

Who is saying what?

These little pictures show you different things that can happen at mealtime. Practise using the Spanish on these two pages, then cover up your book so you can only see these pictures. Now see if you can say what everyone is saying in Spanish. Remember you can check your answers on page 45.

Your hobbies

These people are talking about their hobbies.

New words

hacer	to do
pintar	to paint
guisar	to cook
la afición	hobby
construir cosas	to make things
bailar	to dance
leer	to read
ver la televisión	to watch TV
tejer	to knit
nadar	to swim
jugar	to play
el deporte	sport
el fútbol	football
el tenis	tennis
la música	music
escuchar	to listen to
el instrumento	instrument
el violín	violin
el piano	piano
por la noche	in the evening
algún(o)/a*	any

hacer (to make or do)

yo hago	I do
tú haces	you do (singular)
usted hace	you do (s polite)
él/ella hace	he/she does
nosotros/as hacemos	we do
vosotros/as hacéis	you do (plural)
ustedes hacen	you do (pl polite)
ellos/ellas hacen	they do

jugar y tocar

When you talk about playing a sport, you say **jugar a** and the name of the sport. **A + el** becomes **al**, e.g. **yo juego al fútbol** (I play football).

To talk about playing an instrument, you say **tocar**, e.g. **yo toco el piano** (I play the piano).

¿Qué te gusta hacer?

Me gusta pintar...

...pero no me gusta guisar.

¿Tienes alguna afición?

Sí, construir cosas...

Y me gusta bailar.

What do you do in the evenings?

¿Qué haces por las noches?

Leo libros...

O veo la televisión y tejo.

*Where in English you ask "Do you have a hobby/play an instrument?", in Spanish you use an extra word: **algún**, and say "Do you have any hobby/play any instrument?"

The sporty type

¿Tienes alguna afición?

Me gusta el deporte.

Yo nado.

Yo juego al fútbol

Y yo juego al tenis.

Music lovers

¿Tienen ustedes aficiones?

Sí, nos gusta escuchar música.

¿Tocan algún instrumento?

Y yo toco el piano.

Sí, yo toco el violín.

What are they doing?

A

B

C

D

E

Cover up the rest of the page and see if you can say what all these people are doing in Spanish, e.g. **Él juega al fútbol.** What are your hobbies?

Telling the time

Here you can find out how to tell the time in Spanish. You can look up any numbers you don't know on page 40.

There is no word for "past" in Spanish; you just add the number of minutes to the hour: **son las nueve y cinco** (it is five past nine). To say "five to" you say **menos cinco** (less five): **son las nueve menos cinco** (it is five to nine).

New words

¿qué hora es?	what is the time?
es la una	it is one o'clock
son las dos	it is two o'clock
menos cinco	five to
y cuarto	quarter past
menos cuarto	quarter to
y media	half past
mediodía	midday
medianoche	midnight
de la mañana	in the morning
de la noche	in the evening
a	at
levantarse	to get up
su	his/her
desayunar	to have breakfast
almorzar	to have lunch
cenar	to have supper
él va	he goes
al colegio	to school
a la cama	to bed

ir (to go)	
yo voy	I go
tú vas	you go (singular)
usted va	you go (s pol)
él/ella va	he/she/it goes
nosotros/as vamos	we go
vosotros/as vais	you go (plural)
ustedes van	you go (pl pol)
ellos/ellas van	they go

What is the time?

Here is how to ask what the time is.

The time is . . .

Son las nueve y cinco.

Son las nueve y cuarto.

Son las nueve y media.

Son las diez menos cuarto.

Son las diez menos cinco.

Es mediodía/ medianoche.

What time of day?

Son las seis de la mañana.

Son las seis de la tarde.

---

26   *For one o'clock, midnight and midday, you use the singular verb, e.g. **es la una y diez** (it is ten past one). For other times of day, you use the plural verb, e.g. **son las tres y cuarto** (it is a quarter past three).

Marcos' day

Read what Marcos does throughout the day, then see if you can match each clock with the right picture. You can find out what the answers are on pages 44-45.

a b c d e f g h

1 Marcos se levanta a las siete y media.*

2 Desayuna a las ocho.

3 A las nueve menos cuarto va al colegio.

4 Almuerza** a las doce y media.

5 A las dos y diez juega al fútbol.

6 A las cinco y cuarto ve la televisión.

7 A las seis cena.

8 Se va a la cama a las ocho y media.

What time is it?

Can you say in Spanish what times these clocks show?

a b c d e f g h i j k l m n o

*Some verbs are formed from two parts. You can read about these on pages 42-43.
To learn more about verbs like **almorzar (verbs that sometimes change letters in their stem), see page 43.

Arranging things

Here is how to arrange things with your friends.

New words

¿vamos . . ?	shall we go . . ?
¿cuándo?	when?
el martes	on Tuesday
por la mañana	in the morning
por la tarde	in the afternoon
por la noche	in the evening
la piscina	swimming pool
hacia	at about
hasta el martes	until Tuesday
hoy	today
hasta mañana	until tomorrow
esta tarde	this evening
de acuerdo	O.K.
no puedo	I can't
no es posible	that's no good
¡qué pena!	it's a pity!
ir a	to go to
el cine	cinema
la fiesta	party

Days of the week

domingo	Sunday
lunes	Monday
martes	Tuesday
miércoles	Wednesday
jueves	Thursday
viernes	Friday
sábado	Saturday

Tennis

Swimming

Going to the cinema

Going to a party

¿Vienes a mi fiesta?

¿Cuándo es?

El sábado por la tarde.

¡Qué pena! No es posible.

El sábado voy a bailar.

Your diary for the week

Here is your diary, showing you what you are doing for a week. Read it, then see if you can answer the questions at the bottom of the page in Spanish.

lunes
16:00 horas. Tenis.

martes
14:00 horas. Piano.
17:30 Piscina.

miércoles
15:00 horas. Tenis.
19:45 Cine.

Jueves

viernes
20:00 Ir a bailar con Jaime.

sabado
14:00 horas. Fútbol.
19:00 horas. Fiesta!

domingo
Tenis por la tarde.

¿Qué haces el viernes?
¿Cuándo juegas al tenis?
¿Cuándo vas al cine?
¿Tocas el piano el jueves?
¿Qué haces el domingo?
¿A qué hora es la fiesta el sábado?

a + el

When **a** comes before **el**, you say **al** instead: **¿vamos al cine?** (shall we go to the cinema?)*

Asking where places are

Here and on the next two pages you can find out how to ask your way around.

New words

perdone	excuse me
de nada	not at all
aquí/allí	here/there
la oficina de correos	post office
en la plaza del mercado	in the market place
el hotel	hotel
después	then
gire . . .	turn . . .
¿hay . . ?	is there . . ?
cerca de aquí	nearby
la calle	street
justo	just
¿está lejos?	is it far?
a cinco minutos	five minutes away
a pie	on foot
el supermercado	supermarket
frente a	opposite
al lado de	next to
el banco	bank
la farmacia	chemist's

How to say "you"

There are four words for "you" in Spanish.* You say **tú** to a friend, but it is more polite to say **usted** to an adult you don't know well. When talking to more than one person you use **vosotros**, or **ustedes** to be more polite.

Directions

todo recto

a la izquierda   **a la derecha**

Being polite

> *Perdone, señor . . .*

> *Gracias.*

> *De nada.*

This is how to say "excuse me". It is best to add **señor, señora** or **señorita**.

When people thank you, it is polite to answer **"De nada"**.

Where is . . ?

> *Perdone, señora, ¿dónde está la oficina de correos?*

> *Allí, en la plaza del mercado.*

> *¿Dónde está el hotel de la estación, por favor?*

> *Gire a la izquierda aquí, después siga todo recto.*

*See pages 42-43.

Is there a . . . nearby?

Is it far?

Perdone, señor, ¿hay un café cerca de aquí?

¿Está lejos?

Sí, justo a la izquierda en la calle Colón.

No, a cinco minutos a pie.

Perdone, señorita, ¿hay un supermercado cerca de aquí?

Sí, allí, frente al banco.

¿Y una farmacia cerca de aquí?

Justo al lado del supermercado.

Other useful places to ask for

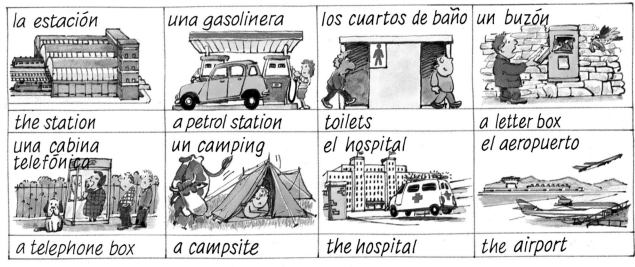

la estación	una gasolinera	los cuartos de baño	un buzón
the station	a petrol station	toilets	a letter box
una cabina telefónica	un camping	el hospital	el aeropuerto
a telephone box	a campsite	the hospital	the airport

31

Finding your way around

Here you can find out how to ask your way around and follow directions. When you have read everything, try the map puzzle on the opposite page.

Perdone, señor,
¿para ir a la estación,
por favor?*

Tome la primera a la derecha, después la segunda a la izquierda.

La estación está a la derecha.

¿Para ir al albergue juvenil, por favor?

Siga todo recto hasta la estación...

después tome la tercera calle a la derecha.

¿Para ir a la oficina de turismo, por favor?

¿En coche?
Continúe todo recto...

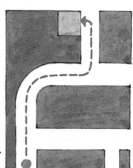

Después tome la primera calle a la izquierda.

*Por favor is the polite way to say "please".

New words

¿para ir a . . ?	how do I get to . . ?	**hasta**	as far as
tome . . .	take . . .	**en coche**	by car
continúe . . .	carry on . . .	**la primera calle**	the first street
el albergue juvenil	youth hostel	**la segunda calle**	the second street
		la tercera calle	the third street
la oficina de turismo	tourist office	**el Ayuntamiento**	town hall
		la iglesia	church

tomar	to take			When people are telling you which way to go, they use the command form of the verb: **Tome . . .** (Take . . .), e.g. **Tome la primera calle . . .**
yo tomo	I take	**nosotros/as tomamos**	we take	
tú tomas	you take (singular)	**vosotros/as tomáis**	you take (plural)	
usted toma	you take (s pol)	**ustedes toman**	you take (pl polite)	
él/ella toma	he/she takes	**ellos/ellas toman**	they take (m/f)	

Finding your way around Bahía

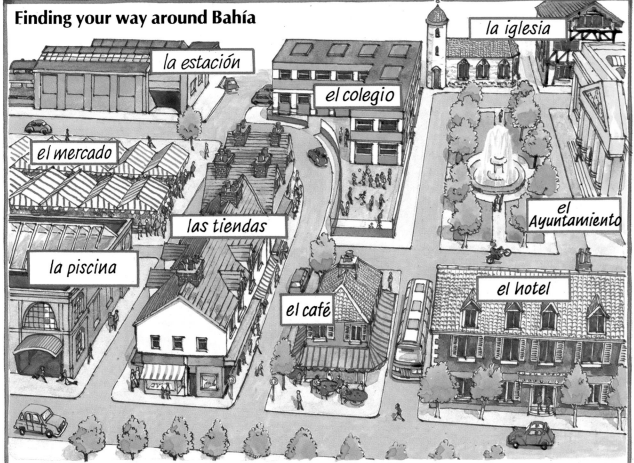

How would you ask someone the way to the market place? How would you ask them if there is a café nearby? Ask how far it is.

Can you tell the person in the yellow car how to get to the church?
Can you direct someone from the hotel to the market?

Where would these directions take the yellow car?
Tome la segunda calle a la izquierda y está a la derecha.

Going shopping

Here and on the next two pages you can find out how to say what you want when you go shopping. When you go into a Spanish shop you should say "**Buenos días, señora**" (or **señor** or **señorita**). If there are lots of people you simply say "**Buenos días**".

Spending money

There are 100 **céntimos** in a **euro**. On price labels, the symbol € is used after the price. For example, **dos euros** is written as **2€**, and **dos euros veinte** as **2,20€**. To understand prices you must know the numbers in Spanish. They are listed on page 40.

New words

ir de compras	to go shopping
comprar	to buy
la panadería	baker's
la tienda de comestibles	grocer's
la carnicería	butcher's
la leche	milk
los huevos	eggs
la fruta	fruit
las verduras	vegetables
la carne	meat
el panecillo	bread roll
la manzana	apple
el tomate	tomato
¿qué desea (usted)?	can I help you?
quiero	I would like
sí, cómo no	with pleasure
¿algo más?	anything else?
¿eso es todo?	is that all?
¿cuánto es?	how much is that?
aquí está/tiene	there you are
un litro	a litre
un kilo	a kilo
medio kilo	half a kilo
entonces	so, well then

Señora Prados goes shopping

La Señora Prados va de compras.

Compra pan en la panadería.

En la panadería

Buenos días, señora.

Buenos días, señora.

Quiero cuatro panecillos.

Sí, cómo no. ¿Algo más?

Tres euros, por favor.

No, gracias. ¿Cuánto es?

¡Aquí tiene! Gracias.

Compra leche y huevos en la tienda de comestibles.

Compra frutas y verduras en el mercado.

Compra carne en la carnicería.

En la tienda de comestibles

En el mercado

More shopping and going to a café

Here you can find out how to ask how much things cost and how to order things in a café.

New words

costar	to cost
¿cuánto cuesta /cuestan?	how much is /are?
la tarjeta postal	postcard
. . . el kilo	. . . a kilo
. . . cada uno/una	. . . each
la rosa	rose
déme siete	give me seven
el café	coffee
la cuenta	the bill
las uvas	grapes
la naranja	orange
el plátano	banana
la piña	pineapple
el limón	lemon
el melocotón	peach
la limonada	lemonade
la coca-cola	coca-cola
el te	tea
con leche	with milk
con limón	with lemon
el chocolate	hot chocolate
un vaso de	a glass of
un helado	ice cream
aquí lo tiene	here it is

Asking how much things cost

¿Cuánto cuesta* esta tarjeta postal?

Sesenta céntimos.

¿Cuánto cuestan las uvas?

Dos euros treinta el kilo.

2,30€

¿Cuánto cuestan las rosas?

Tres euros diez cada una.

3,10€

Entonces, déme siete, por favor.

Going to a café

¿Qué desea?

Un café, por favor.

¡Aquí lo tiene!

Gracias.

La cuenta, por favor.

Son tres euros.

*To learn more about verbs like **costar** (verbs that sometimes change letters in their stem), see pages 42-43.

Buying fruit

Everything on the fruit stall is marked with its name and price.

Look at the picture, then see if you can answer the questions below it.

MANZANAS 1,80€ el kilo

¿Qué desea usted?

PLÁTANOS 1,70€ el kilo

UVAS 2,30€ el kilo

NARANJAS 1,90€ el kilo

PIÑAS 2€ cada una

MELO-COTONES 2,10€ el kilo

LIMONES 0,40€ cada uno

How do you tell the stallholder you would like four lemons, a kilo of bananas and a pineapple? How much do each of these things cost?

¿Qué cuesta dos euros cada una?
¿Qué cuesta dos euros diez el kilo?
¿Qué cuesta dos euros treinta el kilo?
¿Qué cuesta cuaranta céntimos?

Things to order

Here are some things you might want to order in a café.

Quiero...

una limonada

una coca-cola

un te con leche

un te con limón

un zumo de naranja

un chocolate

un vaso de leche

un helado

The months and seasons

Here you can learn what the seasons and months are called and find out how to say what the date is.

New words

el mes	month
el año	year
¿cuál es la fecha?	what is the date?
hoy	today
el cumpleaños	birthday

The seasons

la primavera	spring
el verano	summer
el otoño	autumn
el invierno	winter

The months

enero	January
febrero	February
marzo	March
abril	April
mayo	May
junio	June
julio	July
agosto	August
septiembre	September
octubre	October
noviembre	November
diciembre	December

The seasons

la primavera

marzo, abril, mayo . . .

el verano

junio, julio, agosto . . .

el otoño.

septiembre, octubre, noviembre . . .

el invierno

diciembre, enero, febrero

First, second, third . . .

primer(o)/a*	first
segundo/a	second
tercer(o)/a*	third
cuarto/a	fourth
quinto/a	fifth
sexto/a	sixth
séptimo/a	seventh
octavo/a	eighth
noveno/a**	ninth
décimo/a	tenth
undécimo/a	eleventh
duodécimo/a	twelfth

To say the date, "the first" is **el primero**, but for all other dates, you just say **el** plus the number.

Enero es el primer mes del año.

Febrero es el segundo mes del año.

Diciembre es el duodécimo mes del año.

Can you say where the rest of the months come in the year?

*When you use **primero** and **tercero** immediately before a masculine singular noun, you shorten them to **primer** and **tercer**.   **There are two words for ninth in Spanish: **noveno/a** and **nono/a**.

What is the date?

Hoy es el tres de mayo.

¿Qué fecha es hoy?

El primero de enero

Writing the date

Madrid, 4 de mayo

Here you can see how a date is written. You put the number, **de** (of) and the month.

When is your birthday?

¿Cuándo es tu cumpleaños?

Es el diez de noviembre.

Mi cumpleaños es el doce de febrero.

El cumpleaños de Simón es el ocho de junio.

When are their birthdays?

The dates of the children's birthdays are written below their pictures. Can you say in Spanish when they are, e.g. **El cumpleaños de Marisa es el dos de abril**.

Marisa	Armando	Elena	Clara	Carlos	Roberto

el 2 de abril	el 21 de junio	el 18 de octubre	el 31 de agosto	el 3 de marzo	el 7 de septiembre

39

Colours and numbers

Colours are describing words, so they end in "o" when they refer to an **el** word and in "a" when they refer to a **la** word. If a colour ends in "e", "a" or in a consonant, the ending doesn't change.

The colours

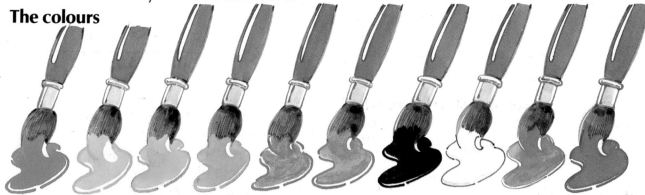

rojo(a)　azul　amarillo(a)　verde　naranja　rosa　negro(a)　blanco(a)　gris　marrón

What colour is it?

Cover the picture above and see if you can say what colour everything is in the painting. You should know all the words you need.*

Numbers

You count the 30s, 40s etc. to the 90s in the same way as 30 to 39: **treinta y uno** (31), **treinta y dos** (32), **treinta y tres** (33), etc.

1	uno	11	once	21	veintiuno
2	dos	12	doce	22	veintidós
3	tres	13	trece	23	veintitrés
4	cuatro	14	catorce	24	veinticuatro
5	cinco	15	quince	25	veinticinco
6	seis	16	dieciséis	26	veintiséis
7	siete	17	diecisiete	27	veintisiete
8	ocho	18	dieciocho	28	veintiocho
9	nueve	19	diecinueve	29	veintinueve
10	diez	20	veinte	30	treinta
				31	treinta y uno
				40	cuarenta

41	cuarenta y uno
50	cincuenta
51	cincuenta y uno
60	sesenta
70	setenta
80	ochenta
90	noventa
100	cien
200	doscientos
300	trescientos
400	cuatrocientos
500	quinientos

Pronunciation guide

In Spanish many letters are pronounced differently. The best way to learn to speak Spanish is to listen carefully to Spanish people and copy what they say, but here are some general points to help you.

Below is a list of letters with a guide to how to pronounce each one. For each Spanish sound we have shown an English word, or part of a word, which sounds like it. Read it out loud in a normal way to find out how to pronounce the Spanish sound, then practise saying the examples shown beneath.

á   A mark like this above a vowel is called a stress mark. It means you should stress this part of the word.

a   Like the "a" sound in "hat": **gracias, casa, vaso**

e   Like the "a" sound in "care": **señor, tener, tres**

i   Like the "ee" sound in "feet": **tía, oficina, amarillo**

o   Like the "o" in "got": **moreno, limón, mayo**

u   Like the "oo" in "moon": **una, lunes, uvas**

ce, ci   Before "i" or "e", "c" is like the "th" in thumb: **alacena, cine**

ca, co, cu   Before other letters it is like the "c" in "cat": **toca, coche, cuenta**

ga, go, gu   Before "a", "o" or "u", "g" sounds like the "g" in "ghost": **gato, agosto, agua**

ge, gi   Before "e" or "i", "g" sounds like the "ch" in "loch": **gente, girar**

gue, gui   Before "ue" or "ui", it is like the "g" in "great" and the "u" is silent: **albergue, guisar**

h   This is never pronounced: so **hombre** sounds like "ombre".

j   This is like the "ch" in "loch": **pájaro, verja, tejer**

ll   Like the "y" in "yes": **lleno, llamar, calle**

ñ   Like the "ni" sound in "onion": **señor, baño, piña**

qu   Like the "k" in "kit", and the "u" is silent: **mantequilla, izquierda, qué**

r, rr   A trilling sound made by putting your tongue behind your upper teeth: **río, marzo, perro**

v/b   "B" and "v" both sound like the "b" in big: **vaso, bailar**

y   When it is alone or at the end of a word "y" is a vowel and it sounds like the "ee" in "feet": **y**

When it comes in the middle of a word, it sounds like the "y" in "yesterday": **mayo**

z   Like the "th" sound in "thunder": **buzón, zumo**

Glossary

Adjectives are shown in their masculine singular form. In general, you change the masculine ending **o** to **a** to make them feminine.

a	at, to
a la derecha	on the right
a la izquierda	on the left
a la orilla del mar	by the sea
a pie	on foot
abril	April
la abuela	grandmother
la abuelita	Granny
el abuelito	Grandad
el abuelo	grandfather
los abuelos	grandparents
la afición	hobby
agosto	August
el agua	water
al lado de	next to
la alacena	cupboard
el albergue juvenil	youth hostel
alemán	German
Alemania	Germany
la alfombra	carpet
¿ algo más ?	anything else ?
algún	any
alguna cosa or algo	something
allí	over there
el almuerzo	lunch
alto	tall
amarillo	yellow
el amigo, la amiga	friend (m/f)
el año	year
el apartamento	flat
aproximadamente	about
aquí	here
el árbol	tree
el armario	wardrobe
arriba	upstairs
el arroz	rice
Austria	Austria
azul	blue
bailar	to dance
el banco	bank
bien	good, well
blanco	white
¡Buen provecho!	Enjoy your meal!
buenas noches	good evening, good night
buenas tardes	good afternoon
buenos días	hello, good morning
buscar	to look for
la butaca	armchair
el buzón	post box
la cabina telefónica	telephone box
cada uno	each (one)
el café	café, coffee

la calle	street
la cama	bed
el camping	campsite
cariñoso	friendly
la carne	meat
la carnicería	butcher's
la casa	house
casi	almost
el castillo	castle
la cena	supper, dinner
cerca de aquí	nearby
la chimenea	chimney
el chocolate	chocolate
el cielo	sky
el cine	cinema
la coca-cola	coca-cola
el coche	car
la cocina	kitchen
cocinar	to cook
el colegio	school
el comedor	dining room
comer	to eat
¿cómo estás?	how are you?
¿cómo te llamas?	what is your name?
comprar	to buy
con	with
construir cosas	to make things
la cortina	curtain
costar(ue)	to cost
¿cuándo?	when?
¿cuánto?	how much?
el cuarto de baño	bathroom
la cuenta	bill
el cumpleaños	birthday
de acuerdo	O.K.
de nada	not at all (in answer to "gracias")
¿de dónde?	from where?
debajo de	under
delante de	in front of
delgado	thin
el deporte	sport
el desayuno	breakfast
después	then
detrás de	behind
diciembre	December
el domingo	Sunday
¿dónde?	where?
el dormitorio	bedroom
el	the (masculine)
en	in
en el campo	in the country
en español	in Spanish
en la ciudad	in the town
encantar	to love, like a lot
encontrar(ue)	to find
enero	January
la ensalada	salad
entonces	then
entre	between

Escocia	Scotland
escuchar	to listen to
los espaguetis	spaghetti
España	Spain
español	Spanish
la estación	station
el estante	bookshelf
esto, esta	this (m/f)
la familia	family
el fantasma	ghost
la farmacia	chemist's
febrero	February
el filete	steak
la flor	flower
Francia	France
frente a	opposite
la fruta	fruit
el fútbol	football
el garaje	garage
la gasolinera	petrol station
el gatito	kitten
el gato	cat
girar	to turn
gracias	thank you
gris	grey
grueso	fat
gustar	to like
hablar	to speak
hacer	to make, to do
la hamburguesa	hamburger
el hámster	hamster
hasta	as far as
hasta la vista	goodbye
hasta pronto	see you soon
hay	there is, there are
el helado	ice cream
la hermana/el hermano	sister/brother
¡Hola!	Hi! Hello!
el hotel	hotel
hoy	today
el huevo	egg
Hungría	Hungary
imposible	that's no good
la India	India
Inglaterra	England
inglés	English
el invierno	winter
ir	to go
ir de compras	to go shopping
el jamón	ham
el jarrón	vase
joven (pl. jóvenes)	young
el jueves	Thursday
jugar(ue)	to play (games)
julio	July
junio	June

el kilo	kilo
la	the (feminine)
la leche	milk
leer	to read
lejos	far
levantarse	to get up
el libro	book
el limón	lemon
la limonada	lemonade
el litro	litre
lo mejor	best
el lunes	Monday
la madre	mother
mal	bad
la mamá	Mum
la mañana	morning
mañana	tomorrow
la mantequilla	butter
la manzana	apple
marrón	brown
el martes	Tuesday
marzo	March
más	more, most
mayo	May
me	me
la medianoche	midnight
el mediodía	noon, midday
mejor	better
el melocotón	peach
menos	less
el mercado	market
el mes	month
la mesa	table
mi, mis	my (singular/plural)
el miércoles	Wednesday
el minuto	minute
mirar	to watch
moreno	dark-haired
mucho	a lot, much, many
muy	very
nadar	to swim
naranja	orange (colour)
la naranja	orange (fruit)
naturalmente	of course
negro	black
el nido	nest
no	no
la noche	evening, night
noviembre	November
o	or
octubre	October
la oficina de correos	post office
la oficina de turismo	tourist office
el otoño	autumn
el padre	father
los padres	parents
el pájaro	bird

el pan	bread	el sofá	sofa
la panadería	baker's	el Sol	sun
el panecillo	bread roll	su	his, hers, its
el papá	Dad	suficiente	enough, quite
las patatas fritas	chips	el supermercado	supermarket
el pastel	cake		
pequeño	small	también	also, too
perdone	excuse me	la tarde	afternoon
el periquito	budgie	la tarjeta postal	postcard
pero	but	la tarta/tarta de frutas	tart/fruit tart
el perrito	puppy	el te	tea
el perro	dog	el tejado	roof
el pescado	fish	tejer	to knit
la peseta	peseta (Spanish money)	el teléfono	telephone
el piano	piano	la televisión	television
la piña	pineapple	tener (ie)	to have
pintar	to paint	tener . . . años	to be . . . years old
la pizza	pizza	tener hambre	to be hungry
la planta	plant	el tenis	tennis
el plátano	banana	tercero	third
la plaza del mercado	market place	la tía	aunt
por favor	please	la tienda de comestibles	grocer's
la primavera	spring	el tío	uncle
primero	first	tocar	to play (instrument)
la puerta	door	todo recto	straight ahead
		tomar	to take
¿qué?	what?	el tomate	tomato
¡qué pena!	it's a pity!	la tortuga	tortoise
el queso	cheese	tu, tus	your (singular/plural)
¿quién?	who?		
¿quieres . . ?	would you like . . ?	un, una	a, an (m,f)
		las uvas	grapes
rojo	red		
la rosa	rose	el vaso	glass (for drinking)
rosa	pink	vender	to sell
rubio	blond	venir (ie)	to come
		la ventana	window
sábado	Saturday	el verano	summer
la sala de estar	living room	verde	green
la salchicha	sausage	la verdura	vegetable
segundo	second	la verja	fence
señor	Mr., Sir	el vestíbulo	hall
señora	Mrs.	viejo	old
señorita	Miss	el viernes	Friday
ser (de)	to be (from)	el violín	violin
la serpiente	snake	vivir	to live
sí	yes		
sí, cómo no	with pleasure	y	and
siempre	always		
sobre	on top of	zumo de naranja	orange juice
sobre todo	best of all		